GALLBLADDER DIET AND COOKBOOK:

Recipes For Breakfast, Lunch, Dinner And More

Dr. Louvenia W. Williamson

TABLE OF CONTENT

CHAPTER ONE

1.0 Understanding the Gallbladder and Its Activities

1.1 Morphology and Function of the Gallbladder

1.2 Reasons and Symptoms of Gallbladder Disease

1.3 Nutritional Adjustments to Promote Gallbladder Health

1.4 Significance of Nutrition in Gallbladder Health

CHAPTER TWO

2.0 Items to Include in a Gallbladder

Diet

2.1 Lean Nutrients

2.2 High-Fiber Meals

2.3 Low-Fat Yogurt Beverages

2.4 Natural Fruits and Vegetables

CHAPTER THREE

3.0 Items to Avoid in a Gallbladder Diet

3.1 High-Fat Meals

3.2 Fried and Greasy Dishes

3.3 Spicy Dishes

3.4 Daily Products with Increased Fat Content

3.5 Caffeine and Alcohol

CHAPTER FOUR

4.0 Menu Preparation for a Gallbladder Diet

4.1 Example Menu Ideas

4.2 Suggestions for Food Planning and Preparation

4.3 Portion Management

CHAPTER FIVE

5.0 Breakfast Recipes for a Gallbladder Plan

5.1 Oatmeal with Mixed Berries

5.2 Cauliflower Omelet

5.3 Smoothies

5.4 Low-Fat Greek Yogurt with Cherries

5.5 Banana Pancakes

CHAPTER SIX

6.0 Brunch Recipes for a Gallbladder Plan

6.1 Roasted Chicken Pesto

6.2 Lentil Broth

6.3 Quinoa and Vegetable Stir-Fry

6.4 Tuna Casserole with Guacamole

6.5 Poultry and Vegetable Wrap

CHAPTER SEVEN

7.0 Supper Recipes for a Gallbladder Plan

7.1 Grilled Mackerel with Marinated Vegetables:

7.2 Poultry Chili:

7.3 Roasted Chicken Breast with Sweet Potato Mash:

7.4 Baked Mackerel with Vegetables

7.5 Grilled Chicken with Sweet Squash

7.6 Vegetable Risotto

7.7 Marinated Scallop Skewers

7.8 Roasted Bell Pepper

CHAPTER EIGHT

8.0 Appetizer Recipes for a Gallbladder Plan

8.1 Apple segments with almond butter

8.2 Apple Slices with Hazelnut Butter

8.3 Hummus and Celery Skewer

8.4 Greek Yogurt with Almonds

8.5 Trail Mix

8.6 Handmade Popcorn

CHAPTER NINE

9.0 Dessert Recipes for a Gallbladder Plan

9.1 Roasted Apples with Cinnamon and Walnuts

9.2 Banana Oatmeal Muffins

9.3 Cherry Sorbet

9.4 Greek Yogurt with Mixed Cherries

9.5 Strawberry Chia Pudding

9.6 Roasted Apples with Cinnamon

9.7 Frozen Sorbet with Mixed Cherries

9.8 Rice Risotto with Cardamom and Raisins

9.9 Black Chocolate-Covered Strawberries

CHAPTER TEN

10.0 Suggestions for Maintaining a Healthy Gallbladder Nutrition

10.1 Keeping Hydrated

10.2 Incorporating Physical Exercise

10.3 Preventing Rapid Weight Reduction or Increase

10.4 Managing Tension

10.5 Routine Physical Check-Ups

All rights reserved. No part of this publication may be reproduced, distributed, or transmitted in any form or by any means, including photocopying, recording, or other electronic or mechanical methods, without the prior written permission of the publisher, except in the case of brief quotations embodied in critical reviews and certain other noncommercial uses permitted by copyright law.

Copyright © (Dr. Louvenia W. Williamson), (2023).

CHAPTER ONE

1.0 Understanding the Gallbladder and Its Activities

The gallbladder is a small, pear-shaped structure situated under the liver in the upper-right part of the abdomen.

It serves an essential part of the digestive system by holding and discharging bile, a substance generated by the liver that helps process lipids.

When food reaches the small intestine, a hormone called cholecystokinin (CCK) is produced, which prompts the gallbladder to constrict and discharge accumulated bile into the small intestine. The bile then serves to break down lipids and receive fat-soluble vitamins, such as vitamins A, D, E, and K.

If the gallbladder is not functioning correctly, it can contribute to the development of gallstones, inflammation of the gallbladder (cholecystitis), or other conditions. Indications of gallbladder difficulties may include gastrointestinal discomfort, nausea, vomiting, and temperature.

Nutritious food can play an essential part in maintaining the health of the gallbladder. Consuming a diet that is low in saturated and fatty fats, high in fiber, and contains plenty of fresh fruits and vegetables can help decrease the chance of developing gallbladder difficulties.

In other words, The gallbladder is an essential component in the digestive system that stores and distributes bile, a substance that serves to break down lipids in the small intestine. The bile is generated by the liver and transmitted to the gallbladder through the hepatic channels. When food reaches the small intestine, the gallbladder is notified to discharge the accumulated bile into the small intestine via the common bile duct.

Bile is made up of water, bile acids, cholesterol, bilirubin, and other components. Bile salts serve an essential role in emulsifying lipids, which means they break down fats into smaller molecules that can be more easily metabolized by enzymes. This procedure increases the surface area of the fat molecules, enabling enzymes to access and break them down more effectively. The decomposition of lipids by bile also helps in the assimilation of fat-soluble vitamins, such as vitamins A, D, E, and K.

If the gallbladder is not functioning correctly, it can lead to the development of gallstones, which are calcified crystals that can cause discomfort and inflammation. Gallstones can develop when the liver includes too much cholesterol, bilirubin, or other substances that can consolidate into stones. Inflammation of the gallbladder, or cholecystitis, can also develop if the bile duct becomes obstructed by a gallstone or if the gallbladder becomes contaminated.

To help prevent gallbladder difficulties, it is essential to maintain a healthy diet that is low in saturated and fatty fats, high in fiber and contains plenty of fresh fruits and vegetables. Consuming plenty of water and keeping refreshed can also help to prevent the development of gallstones. Frequent exercise and maintaining a healthy weight can also help decrease the chance of gallbladder difficulties. If you experience indications of gallbladder difficulties, such as abdominal discomfort, nausea, vomiting, or temperature, it is essential to consult with a healthcare practitioner.

1.1 Morphology and Function of the Gallbladder

The gallbladder is a tubular structure that stores and discharges bile, which is a substance generated by the liver.
The gallbladder has three major parts: the fundus, the stomach, and the spine. The fundus is the spherical section at the apex of the gallbladder, the body is the major component of the organ, and the neck is the narrow part that attaches to the cystic duct. The cystic duct is the conduit that transports bile from the gallbladder to the common bile duct, which then distributes the bile to the small intestine.

The gallbladder serves as an essential part of the digestive system by holding and discharging bile. Bile is generated by the liver and is made up of water, bile acids, cholesterol, bilirubin, and other components. Bile serves to break down lipids in the small intestine by emulsifying them into smaller molecules, which makes them simpler to process by enzymes. Saliva also serves to assimilate fat-soluble vitamins, such as vitamins A, D, E, and K.

When food reaches the small intestine, a hormone called cholecystokinin (CCK) is produced. CCK prompts the gallbladder to constrict and discharge accumulated bile into the small intestine through the cystic duct. The bile helps to process the lipids in the diet and receive the fat-soluble micronutrients.

If the gallbladder is not functioning correctly, it can contribute to the development of gallstones, inflammation of the gallbladder, or other conditions. Indications of gallbladder difficulties may include gastrointestinal discomfort, nausea, vomiting, and temperature. In some instances, the operation to remove the gallbladder, known as a cholecystectomy, may be essential to address gallbladder disorders.

The activities of the gallbladder include:

1. **Bile storage:** The liver generates bile consistently, but it is retained and concentrated in the gallbladder. This serves to increase the strength of the bile and make it more efficient in breaking down lipids.

2. **Bile release:** When fatty meals reach the small intestine, the gallbladder compresses and discharges bile into the small intestine through the cystic duct. The bile serves to coagulate lipids, making them simpler to process and assimilate.

3. **Fat digestion:** Bile salts in the bile break down fat into smaller molecules, which increases their

surface area and makes them more approachable to digestive enzymes. This procedure, known as emulsification, enables the enzymes to break down the lipids more efficiently and effectively.

4. **Absorption of fat-soluble vitamins:** Bile also assists in the absorption of fat-soluble vitamins such as vitamins A, D, E, and K. These vitamins require fat to be ingested, and bile serves to coagulate the lipids, making the vitamins accessible for absorption.

5. **Garbage elimination:** Bile also serves to eradicate waste products such as bilirubin, a consequence of the decomposition of red blood cells. Excess bilirubin can contribute to jaundice, a condition distinguished by discoloration of the skin and eyes.

Overall, the gallbladder serves a critical part in the metabolism and assimilation of lipids and fat-soluble micronutrients. It also helps to eradicate waste products from the body. If the gallbladder is not functioning correctly, it can contribute to the development of gallstones, inflammation, and other complications.

1.2 Reasons and Symptoms of Gallbladder Disease

Gallbladder disease refers to a variety of conditions that impact the gallbladder, including inflammation, infection, and the development of gallstones. The reasons and symptoms of gallbladder illness can differ depending on the particular situation. Here are some of the most prevalent reasons and symptoms of gallbladder disease:

Causes:

1. **Gallstones:** The most prevalent cause of gallbladder illness is the development of gallstones, which are solid collections of bile that can obstruct the passage of bile from the gallbladder.

2. **Biliary dyskinesia:** This condition happens when the gallbladder does not constrict correctly, which can cause bile to build up in the gallbladder and increase the chance of gallstones.

3. **Inflammation:** Inflammation of the gallbladder, known as cholecystitis, can be caused by an obstruction of the bile duct or an infection.

4. **Inflammation:** Infection of the gallbladder, known as cholangitis, can be caused by microbes invading the bile duct.

Symptoms:

1. **Gastrointestinal discomfort:** The most prevalent indication of gallbladder illness is a pain in the upper right or center of the abdomen, which can be acute or mild.

2. **Nausea and vomiting:** Many individuals with gallbladder illness experience nausea and vomiting, which may be accompanied by gastrointestinal discomfort.

3. **Fever and shivers:** Inflammation of the gallbladder can produce a temperature and chills.

4. **Jaundice:** If the bile duct becomes obstructed, it can cause an accumulation of bilirubin in the blood, which can contribute to jaundice, a

condition distinguished by discoloration of the skin and eyes.

5. **Variations in stool movements:** Gallbladder illness can produce changes in digestive movements, such as diarrhea or constipation.

6. **Indigestion:** Some individuals with gallbladder disease may experience indigestion, swelling, or flatulence after consuming greasy meals.

Overall, the symptoms of gallbladder illness can range from minor to serious and may require medical treatment depending on the underlying condition. It is essential to obtain medical assistance if you experience any of these symptoms.

1.3 Nutritional Adjustments to Promote Gallbladder Health

Maintaining a healthy diet is important for maintaining gallbladder health, particularly if you have a history of gallstones or other gallbladder problems. Here are some nutritional adjustments that can help promote gallbladder health:

1. **Minimize saturated and trans fats:** Excessive consumption of saturated and trans fats can increase the chance of gallstones and other gastrointestinal disorders. Instead, concentrate on consuming healthful lipids, such as those found in almonds, grains, and fatty seafood.

2. **Increase fiber intake:** A diet rich in fiber can help to prevent constipation, which can increase the chance of gallstones. Strive

for at least 25 grams of fiber per day, which can be received from fruits, vegetables, whole cereals, and legumes.

3. **Consume plenty of water:** Keeping hydrated is essential for maintaining healthy biliary production and preventing the development of gallstones. Strive for at least eight containers of water per day.

4. **Reduce alcohol intake:** Inappropriate alcohol consumption can increase the chance of gallbladder disease and should be avoided or restricted.

5. **Consume smaller, more frequent meals:** Consuming smaller, more frequent meals throughout the day can help to prevent the accumulation of acid in the gallbladder, which can increase the risk of gallstones.

6. **Prevent quick weight loss:** Speedy weight reduction can increase the chance of gallstones and other gastrointestinal disorders. Instead, strive for gradual, steady weight reduction through healthful nutrition and frequent activity.

7. **Consume a balanced diet:** A balanced diet that includes a selection of fruits, vegetables, lean protein, and healthy lipids can help to support general gallbladder health.

Overall, adopting nutritional adjustments to promote gallbladder health can be a straightforward and effective way to decrease the chance of gallstones and other gallbladder difficulties.

1.4 Significance of Nutrition in Gallbladder Health

The gallbladder serves an essential role in metabolism by holding and producing bile, a substance that helps to break down lipids in the small intestine. As such, maintaining a healthy diet is important for supporting gallbladder health and preventing the development of gallstones and other gallbladder problems.

Here are some of the reasons why nutrition is essential for gallbladder health:

1. **Prevents the formation of gallstones:** One of the most prevalent gallbladder disorders is the development of gallstones, which are hardened collections of bile. Consuming a diet that is high in fiber and low in saturated and fatty fats can help to prevent the development of gallstones.

2. **Promotes healthy bile production:** Bile generation is important for normal metabolism and the decomposition of lipids in the small intestine. Consuming a diet that is high in healthy lipids, such as those found in almonds, grains, and fatty seafood can help to promote healthy bile production.

3. **Decrease inflammation:** Inflammation of the gallbladder, known as cholecystitis, can be caused by an obstruction of the bile duct or an infection. Consuming a diet that is high in anti-inflammatory foods, such as fruits, vegetables, whole cereals, and lean protein, can help to decrease inflammation and promote gallbladder health.

4. **Maintains healthy weight:** Obesity and quick weight reduction are both risk factors for gallbladder illness.

Consuming a healthy, balanced diet and maintaining a healthy weight through frequent exercise can help to decrease the chance of gallbladder difficulties.

5. **Promotes overall digestive health:** Consuming a diet that is high in fiber, lean protein, and healthy lipids can help to support overall digestive health, which is important for gallbladder health.

Ultimately, the significance of nutrition in gallbladder health cannot be emphasized. By making healthy nutritional decisions and choosing a balanced, nourishing diet, you can help to prevent the development of gallstones and other gallbladder problems, and support general intestinal health.

CHAPTER TWO

2.0 Items to Include in a Gallbladder Diet

A gallbladder diet generally includes foods that are low in fat and high in fiber, as well as foods that can help to decrease inflammation and promote healthy bile production. These meals can help to prevent the development of gallstones and other gallbladder problems, and support general intestinal health.

Some of the items that are frequently included in a gallbladder diet include:

1. **Fruits and vegetables:** Fruits and vegetables are rich in fiber, which can help to prevent constipation and decrease the chance of gallstones. They are

also abundant in vitamins, minerals, and antioxidants, which can help to decrease inflammation and promote general health.

2. **Lean protein:** Lean protein options such as poultry, seafood, and tofu are reduced in fat and can help to promote optimal bile production.

3. **Whole carbohydrates:** Whole grains such as brown rice, quinoa, and whole wheat bread are rich in fiber and can help to prevent constipation.

4. **Beneficial lipids:** Healthy fats such as those found in almonds, seeds, avocado, and fatty seafood can help to promote healthy liver production and decrease inflammation.

5. **Water:** Keeping refreshed is essential for maintaining healthy biliary production and preventing

the development of gallstones.

It is also essential to avoid foods that can exacerbate gallbladder difficulties, such as those that are rich in saturated and toxic fats, cholesterol, and processed carbohydrates. These include cooked foods, heavy meats, manufactured foods, and sweetened beverages.

Generally, a gallbladder diet should be centered on whole, nutrient-dense meals that can help to support gallbladder health and encourage overall well-being.

2.1 Lean Nutrients

Lean proteins are an essential component of a gallbladder diet, as they are low in fat and can help to promote healthy bile production. Here are some instances of lean nutrients and their benefits:

1. **Poultry:** Chicken is a lean protein that is low in cholesterol and high in protein, making it a perfect choice for those with gallbladder problems. Poultry also includes necessary amino acids that are important for maintaining muscular strength and supporting general health.

2. **Fish:** Healthy seafood such as salmon, tuna, and mackerel are rich in omega-3 fatty acids, which can help to decrease inflammation and promote healthy liver production. This seafood is also reduced in saturated fat and can help to decrease triglyceride levels.

3. **Tofu:** Tofu is a vegetarian protein option that is low in fat and high in protein. It is also high in isoflavones, which have been shown to have anti-inflammatory characteristics.

4. **Beans:** Beans are an excellent source of vegetarian protein and are rich in fiber, which can help to prevent constipation and decrease the risk of gallstones. They are also reduced in oil and can help to decrease triglyceride levels.

5. **Egg whites:** Egg whites are low in cholesterol and high in protein, making them a decent option for those with gastrointestinal problems. They are also an excellent supply of important amino acids and can help to preserve muscular development.

When selecting lean proteins, it is essential to avoid high-fat types of meat such as beef, pork, and lamb. Processed meats such as bacon and sausage should also be avoided, as they are high in fat and sodium. Instead, choose lean portions of beef and chicken and opt for grilled, roasted, or sautéed preparations.

Vegetarian sources of protein such as tofu, legumes, and lentils are also excellent choices for those following a gallbladder diet.

2.2 High-Fiber Meals

High-fiber meals are an essential component of a gallbladder diet, as they can help to prevent constipation and decrease the chance of gallstones. Here are some instances of high-fiber meals and their benefits:

1. **fruits**: Fruits such as apples, pears, and cherries are rich in fiber and can help to encourage frequent digestive movements. They are also abundant in vitamins, minerals, and antioxidants, which can help to decrease inflammation and promote general health.

2. **Vegetables:** Vegetables such as cauliflower, carrots, and verdant greens are rich in fiber and can help to prevent constipation. They are also minimal in nutrients and abundant in nutrition, making them an essential component of a nutritious diet.

3. **Whole carbohydrates:** Whole grains such as brown rice, quinoa, and whole wheat bread are rich in fiber and can help to prevent constipation. They are also abundant in vitamins, minerals, and antioxidants, which can help to decrease inflammation and promote general health.

4. **Nuts and seeds:** Nuts and seeds such as almonds, chia seeds, and flaxseeds are high in fiber and can help to promote regular bowel movements. They are also high in healthful lipids, which can help to decrease

inflammation and promote healthy liver production.

5. **Legumes:** Legumes such as legumes, lentils, and chickpeas are rich in fiber and can help to prevent constipation. They are also an excellent source of vegetarian protein and can help to reduce triglyceride levels.

When increasing your consumption of high-fiber meals, it is essential to do so gradually and consume plenty of water to help prevent constipation. It is also essential to avoid processed carbohydrates such as white bread and spaghetti, as these can contribute to constipation and other intestinal problems. Instead, choose whole grain replacements and incorporate a diversity of high-fiber meals into your diet to support intestinal health.

2.3 Low-Fat Yogurt Beverages

Low-fat dairy products are essential components of a gallbladder diet because they provide a decent supply of calcium and protein without the additional lipids that can cause gallbladder irritation. Here are some examples of low-fat dairy products that can be included in a gallbladder diet:

1. **Skim milk:** Skim milk is an excellent provider of calcium and vitamin D, and it is minimal in calories. It can be used in milkshakes, porridge, or as a refreshment on its own.

2. **Low-fat yogurt:** Low-fat yogurt is an excellent source of protein and calcium, and it can be savored as a refreshment or used in recipes as a replacement for sour cream or mayonnaise.

3. **Cottage cheese:** Cottage cheese is a low-fat, high-protein dairy product that can be used as a refreshment or as a replacement for ricotta cheese in recipes.

4. **Reduced-fat cheese:** Reduced-fat cheese is an excellent source of protein and calcium, and it can be used in recipes that call for cheese, such as omelets, salads, and sandwiches.

It is essential to study labels and choose products that are low in fat and calories, as some low-fat dairy products may still contain high quantities of sugar or other chemicals.

Beneficial Fats and Oils

Beneficial lipids and oils are important components of a gallbladder diet, as they can help to decrease inflammation and promote healthy bile production. Here are some instances of healthful lipids and oils and their benefits:

- **Olive oil:** Olive oil is a rich source of polyunsaturated lipids, which can help to decrease inflammation and promote healthy cholesterol levels. It is also an excellent source of antioxidants, which can help to safeguard against environmental damage.

- **Avocado:** Avocado is a rich source of healthy lipids, including monounsaturated and polyunsaturated fats, which can help to decrease inflammation and promote healthy liver production. It is also an excellent source of fiber and minerals, making it an essential component of a nutritious diet.

- **Fatty fish:** Fatty fish such as salmon, anchovies, and tuna are abundant sources of omega-3 fatty acids, which can help to decrease inflammation and promote healthy liver production. They are also an excellent source of protein, making them an essential component of a balanced diet.

- **Almonds and seeds:** Nuts and seeds such as almonds, walnuts, chia seeds, and flaxseeds are abundant sources of healthy lipids, which can help to decrease inflammation and promote healthy liver production. They are also an excellent source of fiber and protein, making them an essential component of a nutritious diet.

- **Coconut oil:** Coconut oil is a rich source of medium-chain triglycerides, which are readily metabolized and can help to promote healthy liver production. It is also an excellent source of antioxidants and may have antimicrobial and anti-fungal characteristics.

2.4 Natural Fruits and Vegetables

Healthy fruits and vegetables are an important component of a gallbladder diet, as they are abundant in vitamins, minerals, fiber, and phytonutrients that support general health and intestinal function. Here are some instances of fresh fruits and vegetables and their benefits:

1. **Leafy greens:** Leafy greens such as spinach, kale, collard greens, and Swiss chard are high in vitamins A, C, and K, as well as folate and fiber. They can help to support healthy metabolism and decrease inflammation.

2. **Cherries:** Berries such as strawberries, blueberries, raspberries, and blackberries are high in antioxidants, which can help to safeguard against environmental damage and inflammation. They are also low in calories and high in fiber, making them an excellent nibble or addition to beverages.

3. **Citrus fruits**: Citrus fruits such as oranges, grapefruits, lemons, and limes are high in vitamin C, which can help to promote healthy immunological function and decrease inflammation. They are also low in calories and high in fiber, making them an excellent addition to salads or as a nibble.

4. **Cruciferous vegetables:** Cruciferous vegetables such as broccoli, cauliflower, Brussels sprouts, and cabbage are high in fiber, vitamins, and minerals,

as well as antioxidants that can help to safeguard against inflammation and other health problems.

5. **Sweet potatoes:** Sweet potatoes are an abundant source of fiber, vitamins, and minerals, including vitamin A, potassium, and magnesium. They are also low in calories and high in phytonutrients, making them an excellent complement to a healthy diet.

When incorporating fresh fruits and vegetables into your diet, strive to choose a diversity of flavors and kinds to ensure that you are receiving a broad range of nutrients. It is also essential to choose organic choices whenever feasible, as conventionally produced produce may contain herbicides and other chemicals that can contribute to inflammation and other health issues.

CHAPTER THREE

3.0 Items to Avoid in a Gallbladder Diet

Certain meals can provoke symptoms of gallbladder disease or contribute to the development of gallstones. Here are some instances of things to avoid in a gallbladder diet:

1. **Cooked foods:** Fried foods are high in dangerous lipids and can be difficult to process, making them a frequent stimulus for gallbladder complaints.

2. **High-fat meats:** Meats such as beef, pork, and lamb are high in saturated fat and can contribute to inflammation and gallstone development.

3. **Dairy products:** Dairy products such as cheese, butter, and ice cream are high in saturated fat and can be difficult to process, making them a frequent stimulus for gallbladder complaints.

4. **Commercial foods:** Processed foods such as crisps, pastries, and sweets are high in dangerous lipids, sugar, and sodium, and can contribute to inflammation and other health problems.

5. **Fiery foods:** Spicy foods can aggravate the digestive system and provoke symptoms of gallbladder disease, particularly if they contain a lot of chile powder, cayenne pepper, or other hot seasonings.

6. **Caffeine:** Caffeine can stimulate the digestive system and provoke gallbladder symptoms, particularly if ingested in large quantities or on an empty

stomach.

7. **Alcohol:** Alcohol can be difficult to metabolize and can contribute to inflammation and other health problems, making it essential to consume in moderation or avoid it completely.

It is also essential to prevent quick weight reduction or catastrophic diets, as these can increase the risk of gallstone development. Instead, concentrate on making incremental adjustments to your food and lifestyle that promote general health and well-being.

3.1 High-Fat Meals

High-fat meals are typically not recommended in a gallbladder diet, as they can contribute to inflammation and the development of gallstones. However, not all lipids are created identically, and some high-fat meals can be advantageous for gallbladder health. Here are some instances of high-fat meals to consider including in a gallbladder diet:

1. **Avocado:** Avocado is a rich source of healthy polyunsaturated lipids, which can help to decrease inflammation and promote healthy digestion.

2. **Almonds and seeds:** Nuts and seeds such as almonds, walnuts, chia seeds, and flaxseeds are high in healthful lipids, fiber, and phytonutrients, making them an excellent addition to a gallbladder diet.

3. **Olive oil:** Olive oil is a rich source of healthful polyunsaturated lipids and phytonutrients, which can help to decrease inflammation and promote general health.

4. **Fatty seafood:** Fatty fish such

as salmon, tuna, and mackerel are high in omega-3 fatty acids, which can help to decrease inflammation and promote a healthy heart and cognitive performance.

5. **Coconut oil:** Coconut oil is an abundant source of medium-chain triglycerides (MCTs), which are a form of healthful fat that can be readily assimilated and used for energy.

While it is essential to include some healthy lipids in a gallbladder diet, it is still important to consume them in proportion and balance them with plenty of fresh fruits, vegetables, and lean proteins. It may also be beneficial to work with a healthcare practitioner or registered nutritionist to establish an individualized gallbladder diet plan that suits your requirements and preferences.

3.2 Fried and Greasy Dishes

Cooked and sticky meals are often high in dangerous lipids, which can contribute to inflammation and the development of gallstones. In a gallbladder diet, it is typically recommended to restrict or eliminate these kinds of meals as much as feasible. Here are some instances of cooked and sticky meals to avoid:

1. **French fries:** French fries are a popular source of excessive lipids, and are often deep-fried in oil.

2. **Fried chicken:** Fried chicken is generally floured and deep-fried, making it a high-fat meal that can be challenging to stomach.

3. **Rapid food:** Many fast food choices such as burgers, chicken sandwiches, and burritos are high in dangerous

lipids and should be avoided in a gallbladder diet.

4. **Pizza:** Pizza is often high in dangerous lipids and can be challenging to stomach due to its high fat and carbohydrate content.

5. **Potato chips and other snack foods:** Snack foods such as potato chips, maize chips, and other cooked munchies are often high in undesirable lipids and chemicals, which can contribute to inflammation and gallstone development.

While it may be challenging to avoid all fried and greasy foods in a gallbladder diet, it is essential to restrict them as much as possible and choose healthier culinary techniques such as barbecuing, roasting, or broiling instead of frying. Collaborating with a healthcare practitioner or registered nutritionist can also be beneficial in establishing an individualized gallbladder diet plan that suits your requirements and preferences.

3.3 Spicy Dishes

Fiery meals can be a stimulus for some individuals with gastrointestinal difficulties. Substances such as chile peppers, cayenne pepper, and black pepper can stimulate the production of bile, which may produce irritation or pain in individuals with gallbladder disease. Additionally, piquant meals may also increase inflammation and discomfort in the intestinal system, which can exacerbate gallbladder complaints. In a gallbladder diet, it is typically recommended to restrict or prevent piquant meals as much as feasible. Here are some instances of piquant meals to avoid:

1. **Hot sauce:** Hot sauce is often high in piquant chilies and can

be a catalyst for individuals with gastrointestinal difficulties.

2. **Chili peppers:** Chili peppers are a prevalent constituent in many piquant meals and should be avoided in a gallbladder diet.

3. **Curry:** Curry is often prepared with a variety of piquant ingredients and should be avoided or restricted in a gallbladder diet.

4. **Salsa:** Salsa can be a healthful condiment choice, but individuals with gallbladder difficulties should choose moderate or low-spice choices to prevent activating symptoms.

While some individuals with gallbladder difficulties may be able to tolerate minor quantities of acidic foods, it is typically recommended to avoid them as much as possible in a gallbladder diet. Collaborating with a healthcare practitioner or registered nutritionist can also be beneficial in establishing an individualized gallbladder diet plan that suits your requirements and preferences.

3.4 Daily Products with Increased Fat Content

Dairy products that are rich in fat can be challenging to process for individuals with gallbladder difficulties. High-fat dairy products contain saturated lipids that can provoke gallbladder symptoms and contribute to the development of gallstones. In a gallbladder diet, it is typically recommended to restrict or eliminate dairy products with high lipid content. Here are some instances of high-fat dairy products to avoid:

1. **Whole milk:** Whole milk includes the greatest quantity of cholesterol among dairy

products and should be avoided in a gallbladder diet.

2. **Cream**: Thick cream and churning cream are rich in fat and should be restricted or avoided in a gallbladder diet.

3. **Cheddar:** Cheese can be a nutritious source of protein, but many varieties are rich in saturated fat and should be restricted in a gallbladder diet.

4. **Ice cream:** Ice cream is a high-fat delicacy that should be shunned in a gallbladder diet.

5. **Sour cream:** Sour cream is rich in fat and should be restricted or avoided in a gallbladder diet.

Individuals with gallbladder difficulties may be able to tolerate low-fat dairy products such as powdered milk, low-fat yogurt, and reduced-fat cheese. It is essential to study product labels attentively and choose low-fat or reduced-fat choices when feasible. Collaborating with a healthcare practitioner or registered nutritionist can also be beneficial in establishing an individualized gallbladder diet plan that suits your requirements and preferences.

3.5 Caffeine and Alcohol

Caffeine and alcohol are two substances that should be restricted or shunned in a gallbladder diet. Both caffeine and alcohol can cause dehydration and contribute to the development of gallstones, which can exacerbate gallbladder complaints. Here are some instances of caffeine and alcohol-containing substances to avoid or restrict in a gallbladder diet:

1. **Coffee:** Coffee includes caffeine, which can stimulate the production of bile and provoke

gallbladder complaints. Individuals with gastrointestinal difficulties may need to restrict or avoid coffee or transition to decaf choices.

2. **Tea:** Like coffee, the tea includes caffeine and may need to be restricted or ignored in a gallbladder diet.

3. **Beverages:** Soda and other effervescent beverages can cause swelling and may contribute to the development of gallstones.

4. **Drinking:** Alcohol can induce dehydration and contribute to the development of gallstones. Individuals with gallbladder difficulties should restrict or avoid alcohol, including beer, wine, and whiskey.

While some individuals with gallbladder difficulties may be able to tolerate minor quantities of caffeine and alcohol, it is typically recommended to restrict or avoid them as much as possible in a gallbladder diet. Collaborating with a healthcare practitioner or registered nutritionist can also be beneficial in establishing an individualized gallbladder diet plan that suits your requirements and preferences.

CHAPTER FOUR

4.0 Menu Preparation for a Gallbladder Diet

Food preparation is an essential element of a gallbladder diet. Preparing meals ahead of time can help ensure that you are receiving the nutrition you need while avoiding items that can provoke gallbladder symptoms. When menu planning a gallbladder diet, it is essential to concentrate on incorporating lean proteins, high-fiber foods, healthy lipids, and fresh fruits and vegetables while restricting or eliminating high-fat, cooked, sticky, salty, and caffeine and alcohol-containing foods.

To get started with food preparation for a gallbladder diet, consider the following tips:

1. **Prepare your meal ahead of time:** Prepare your recipes for the week ahead of time, taking into consideration your timetable and preferences.

2. **Choose lean proteins:** Incorporate lean proteins such as skinless chicken breast, poultry, seafood, tofu, and lentils into your meals.

3. **Include high-fiber foods:** Incorporate high-fiber foods such as whole cereals, fruits, and vegetables into your meals to promote healthy digestion.

4. **Use healthy lipids:** Use healthy fats such as olive oil, avocado, almonds, and seeds in your foods in proportion.

5. **Prevent high-fat foods:** Restrict or avoid high-fat foods such as cooked foods, sticky foods, and high-fat dairy

products.

6. **Experiment with novel recipes:** Search for recipes that are low in calories and incorporate healthful ingredients that you appreciate.

7. **Remain moistened:** Consume plenty of water throughout the day to stay refreshed and promote healthy digestion.

By following these guidelines and working with a healthcare practitioner or registered nutritionist, you can establish a food plan that suits your particular requirements and inclinations while supporting gallbladder health.

4.1 Example Menu Ideas

For example, meal plans can be a valuable resource when beginning a gallbladder diet. These recipes can provide inspiration and direction on how to structure your meals to incorporate lean proteins, high-fiber foods, healthy lipids, and fresh fruits and vegetables while restricting or eliminating high-fat, cooked, glutinous, salty, and caffeine and alcohol-containing foods. Here are some example meal ideas for a gallbladder diet:

Example Menu Plan 1:

Breakfast: Granola with fresh cherries, shredded walnuts, and a sprinkling of honey

Snack: Apple pieces with coconut butter

Lunch: Turkey and avocado sandwich with whole grain flatbread, chopped cucumbers, and baby arugula

Snack: Zucchini spears with mayonnaise

Dinner: Roasted chicken breast with sautéed sweet potato and green asparagus

Dessert: Roasted pear with a scattering of cinnamon and a spoonful of Greek yogurt

Example Meal Plan 2:

Breakfast: Scrambled eggs with spinach, chopped tomatoes, and whole-grain bread

Snack: Greek yogurt with chopped walnuts and fresh cherries

Lunch: Black bean broth with a mixed greens salad served with roasted chicken breast, sliced avocado, and cherry tomatoes

Snack: Grilled chickpeas

Dinner: Roasted salmon with couscous and sautéed vegetables

Dessert: Roasted apple pieces with a

scattering of cinnamon and a sprinkling of maple syrup

These example menu arrangements can be modified to suit your particular requirements and inclinations. It's essential to consult with a healthcare practitioner or registered nutritionist to establish an individualized food plan that supports your gallbladder health.

4.2 Suggestions for Food Planning and Preparation

In addition to following a gallbladder-friendly meal plan, some suggestions for food planning and preparation can make the process simpler and more pleasurable. Here are some suggestions to consider:

- **Maintain a food notebook:** Keeping a food journal can help you identify items that activate your gallbladder symptoms and monitor your improvement over time.

- **for ingredients in advance:** Preparing your recipes ahead of time and purchasing ingredients in advance can save time and decrease tension.

- **Assemble ingredients ahead of time:** Prepare vegetables, boil cereals, and prepare proteins ahead of time to make dinner preparation simpler during the week.

- **Prepare large quantities of food:** Contemplate preparing bigger volumes of food and preserve individual portions for quick and simple dinners later on.

- **Use a slow cooker or pressure cooker:** Slow cookers and pressure cookers can be beneficial instruments for preparing dishes in preparation and saving time.

- **Experiment with different culinary methods:** Attempt different culinary techniques such as barbecuing, roasting, or baking to add variation to your dinners.

- **Get inventive with herbs and spices:** Experiment with different herbs and spices to add flavor to your dishes without introducing additional oil or sodium.

By following these guidelines, you can make food planning and preparation simpler and more pleasurable while supporting your gallbladder health. Remember to always work with a healthcare practitioner or registered nutritionist to establish an individualized food plan that suits your requirements and preferences.

4.3 Portion Management

Quantity management is an essential element of a healthful gallbladder diet. Consuming too much food, even if it's nutritious, can lead to overwhelming the digestive system and activating gallbladder symptoms such as discomfort, inflammation, and vertigo. Here are some suggestions for exercising portion control:

Use smaller dishes: Using smaller plates can help deceive your brain into believing you're consuming a bigger quantity.

- **Measure your food:** Use measuring containers or a food scale to measure out appropriate serving amounts for your dinners.

- **Observe portion sizes:** Give attention to serving sizes stated on product packages and attempt to adhere to them.

- **Consume carefully:** Consuming leisurely and digesting your meal completely can help you feel satisfied quicker and prevent overloading.

- **Adhere to your body:** Give attention to your body's appetite and satisfaction indications and cease consuming when you feel fulfilled.

- **Prevent interruptions while dining:** Consuming while preoccupied, such as watching TV or using your phone, can contribute to thoughtless eating and overeating.

- **Exercise mindful eating:** Practice mindful eating by enjoying your food, consuming leisurely, and giving attention to the flavors, textures, and scents of your food.

By exercising portion control, you can

support your gallbladder health by preventing overloading and decreasing the probability of activating symptoms.

CHAPTER FIVE

5.0 Breakfast Recipes for a Gallbladder Plan

Breakfast is an essential dish for anyone following a gallbladder diet. It provides the body with the energy and nutrition it needs to start the day and can help prevent overloading later on. A gallbladder-friendly breakfast should be low in cholesterol, high in fiber, and contain lean protein. Here are some instances of breakfast preparations that meet this criterion:

1. **Overnight oatmeal with fruit and nuts:** Incorporate cereals, almond milk, chia seeds, and a small quantity of honey in a container and refrigerate overnight. In the morning, add fresh fruit and shredded

almonds for additional flavor and structure.

2. **Vegetable omelet:** Blend two eggs with a small quantity of milk and prepare in a non-stick saucepan. Incorporate your preferred vegetables, such as spinach, bell peppers, and mushrooms, for additional fiber and nutrients.

3. **Greek yogurt with fruit and granola:** Choose a low-fat Greek yogurt and add fresh cherries or chopped fruit and a small quantity of low-fat granola for additional texture.

4. **Smoothie bowl**: Combine frozen fruit, a small quantity of almond milk, and a sprinkle of protein powder for a nutrient-dense and fulfilling breakfast.

5. **Avocado toast with egg:** Broil a piece of whole-grain bread and top with pureed avocado and a scrambled or cooked egg for a protein-packed breakfast.

By incorporating these gallbladder-friendly breakfast recipes into your diet plan, you can start your day off on the right foot and support your gallbladder health. Remember to always work with a healthcare practitioner or registered nutritionist to establish an individualized food plan that suits your requirements and preferences.

5.1 Oatmeal with Mixed Berries

Recipe: Granola with Mixed Berries

Ingredients:

- 1 cup old-fashioned toasted oats

- 2 tablespoons water

- 1/4 tsp salt

- 1 tbsp honey or maple sugar

- 1/2 tsp cinnamon

- 1/2 cup fresh fruit (such as cherries, sliced banana, or shredded apple)

Possible toppings: chopped almonds, preserved fruit, powdered coconut

Instructions:

1. In a medium-sized saucepan, bring water and salt to a simmer.

2. Toss in powdered oats and decrease the heat to a simmer.

3. Simmer for 5-7 minutes, swirling periodically, until the oats are delicate and the concoction has thickened.

4. Remove from fire and whisk in honey or maple syrup and cinnamon.

5. Divide porridge into dishes and cover with fresh fruit and any preferred garnishes.

6. Consume immediately.

Providing suggestions:

- Garnish with a spoonful of basic Greek yogurt for extra nutrition and smoothness.

- Sprinkle with additional honey or maple syrup for extra sweetness.

- Consume a container of low-fat milk or unsweetened coconut milk for extra nutrients.

Benefits:

- Grains are an excellent source of dietary fiber, which can help reduce triglyceride levels and promote metabolism.

- Natural fruit adds vitamins, minerals, and antioxidants to the meal, which can help improve general health.

- This meal is low in cholesterol and high in fiber and can help support a healthy gallbladder diet.

5.2 Cauliflower Omelet

Recipe: Vegetable Omelet

Ingredients:

- 2 giant embryos
- 1/4 cup shredded assorted vegetables (such as bell pepper, onion, and tomato) (such as bell pepper, onion, and tomato)
- 1 tbsp chopped fresh herbs (such as parsley, basil, or scallions) 1/4 tsp salt
- 1/8 tsp black pepper
- 1 tsp olive oil

Instructions:

1. In a small dish, blend eggs, salt, and black pepper until well-combined.

2. Prepare a nonstick saucepan over medium heat and add olive oil.

3. Once the oil is heated, add the chopped vegetables to the saucepan and simmer for 2-3 minutes, until slightly softened.

4. Spread the egg concoction over the vegetables and use a utensil to distribute it equally in the skillet.

5. Simmer for 2-3 minutes, until the sides of the omelet start to firm.

6. Use a utensil to delicately divide the omelet in half.

7. Continue heating for an additional 1-2 minutes, \ until the omelet is heated through and faintly colored on both sides.

8. Distribute chopped herbs on top of the frittata.

9. Use a spatula to carefully transfer the omelet to a plate and serve immediately.

Providing suggestions:

- Serve with a portion of whole-grain bread or a small helping of fresh fruit for extra fiber and nutrients.

- Garnish with a spoonful of low-fat vanilla Greek yogurt or a scattering of shredded cheese for additional flavor and nutrition.

- Relish as a quick and simple breakfast or small supper.

Benefits:

1. This recipe is rich in protein and low in fat, making it a perfect option for a gallbladder-friendly diet.

2. The vegetables provide a variety of vitamins and minerals, while

the eggs offer additional protein and nutrition.

3. This recipe is simple to personalize with your favorite vegetables and seasonings for a delectable and nourishing dinner.

5.3 Smoothies

Recipe: Fruit Milkshake

Ingredients:

- 1 cup assorted frozen berries (such as strawberries, blueberries, and blackberries) (such as strawberries, blueberries, and raspberries)

- 1/2 cup low-fat basic Greek yogurt

- 1/2 cup unsweetened almond

milk

- 1/2 banana, chopped

- 1 tsp honey (optional)

Instructions:

1. Put all ingredients in a blender and puree until creamy.

2. If the smoothie is too viscous, add additional coconut milk until desired consistency is achieved.

3. Taste and modify sweetness

with honey, if required.

4. Strain into a tumbler and serve immediately.

Providing suggestions:

- Garnish with a scattering of granola or crushed almonds for additional crispness and substance.

- Toss a fistful of broccoli or greens for additional nutrition and nutrients.

- Consume as a quick and simple breakfast or refreshment.

Benefits:

1. This beverage is high in fiber and protein, making it a satisfying and nourishing dinner or refreshment choice.

2. The cherries provide antioxidants and other

advantageous nutrients, while the Greek yogurt provides microorganisms for digestive health.

3. Almond milk is an excellent source of calcium and Vitamin D and is lower in cholesterol than dairy milk, making it a good option for a gallbladder-friendly diet.

4 This recipe can be simply personalized with your preferred fruits and seasonings for a delectable and nutritious cocktail.

Recipe: Vegetable Milkshake

Ingredients:

- 1 cup chopped young broccoli
- 1/2 banana, chopped
- 1 /2 cup frozen pineapple pieces

- 1/2 cup unsweetened almond milk

- 1/2 cup low-fat basic Greek yogurt

Instructions:

1. Put all ingredients in a blender and puree until creamy.

2. If the smoothie is too viscous, add additional coconut milk until desired consistency is achieved.

3. Strain into a tumbler and serve immediately.

Providing suggestions:

- Garnish with a few pieces of fresh fruit or a scattering of chia seeds for additional nutrients.

- Add a tablespoon of peanut butter or almond butter for additional nutrition and flavor.

- Consume as a nutritious and invigorating breakfast or refreshment.

Benefits:

1. This smoothie is filled with nutrition from spinach and strawberries, while Greek yogurt provides protein and microorganisms for digestive health.

2. Almond milk is an excellent source of calcium and Vitamin D and is lower in cholesterol than dairy milk, making it a good

option for a gallbladder-friendly diet.

3. This recipe is a wonderful way to smuggle some additional vegetables and fruits into your diet deliciously and simply.

Recipe: Tropical Milkshake

Ingredients:

- 1/2 cup frozen mango pieces
- 1/2 cup frozen pineapple pieces
- 1/2 banana, chopped
- 1/2 cup low-fat basic Greek yogurt
- 1/2 cup unsweetened coconut cream

Instructions:

1. Put all ingredients in a blender and puree until creamy.

2. If the milkshake is too viscous, add additional coconut

Recipe: Fruit Explosion Smoothie

Ingredients:

- 1 cup thawed mixed berries (strawberries, blueberries, raspberries) (strawberries, blueberries, raspberries)

- 1/2 banana, chopped

- 1/2 cup low-fat vanilla Greek yogurt

- 1/2 cup unsweetened almond milk

- 1 teaspoonful honey

Instructions:

1. Put all ingredients in a blender and puree until creamy.

2. If the smoothie is too viscous, add additional coconut milk until desired consistency is achieved.

3. Strain into a tumbler and serve immediately.

Providing suggestions:

- Garnish with a scattering of granola or a few fresh cherries for additional structure and flavor.

- Add a fistful of spinach for an additional boost of nutrition without impacting the flavor.

- Consume as a nutritious and fulfilling breakfast or refreshment.

Benefits:

1. This beverage is high in antioxidants and fiber from mixed berries, which can help prevent inflammation and promote intestinal health.

2. Greek yogurt and almond milk provide protein and calcium, while honey provides natural deliciousness without introducing artificial sugar.

3. This recipe is a delectable way to incorporate more veggies into your diet while remaining loyal to a gallbladder-friendly food plan.

Recipe: Vegetable Vitality Smoothie

Ingredients:

- 1 banana, divided
- 1 cup green spinach stalks
- 1/2 avocado, skinned and sliced
- 1/2 cup unsweetened almond milk
- 1 teaspoonful of chia seeds
- 1 teaspoonful of honey (optional)

Instructions:

1. Put all ingredients in a blender and puree until creamy.

2. If the smoothie is too viscous, add additional coconut milk until desired consistency is achieved.

3. Strain into a tumbler and serve immediately.

Providing suggestions:

- Garnish with a scattering of hemp seeds or additional chia seeds for extra nutrition and texture.

- Use thawed spinach or add a fistful of ice crystals for a chilled beverage.

- Consume as a nutrient-packed breakfast or refreshment.

Benefits:

1. This beverage is filled with fiber and phytonutrients from the spinach and chia seeds, which can help support healthy digestion and decrease inflammation in the body.

2. Avocado provides healthful lipids and smoothness, while banana contributes natural sweetness and potassium.

3. This recipe is a delectable way to incorporate more vegetables into your diet while following a

gallbladder-friendly food plan.

Recipe: Fruit Explosion Smoothie

Ingredients:

- 1 cup assorted frozen berries (such as strawberries, blueberries, and blackberries) (such as strawberries, blueberries, and raspberries)

- 1/2 cup unsweetened almond milk

- 1/2 cup basic low-fat Greek yogurt

- 1 teaspoonful of honey (optional)

seeds for extra nutrition and texture.

- Use thawed spinach or add a fistful of ice crystals for a chilled beverage.

- Consume as a nutrient-packed breakfast or refreshment.

Benefits:

1. This beverage is filled with fiber and phytonutrients from the spinach and chia seeds, which can help support healthy digestion and decrease inflammation in the body.

2. Avocado provides healthful lipids and smoothness, while banana contributes natural sweetness and potassium.

3. This recipe is a delectable way to incorporate more vegetables into your diet while following a

gallbladder-friendly food plan.

Recipe: Fruit Explosion Smoothie

Ingredients:

- 1 cup assorted frozen berries (such as strawberries, blueberries, and blackberries) (such as strawberries, blueberries, and raspberries)

- 1/2 cup unsweetened almond milk

- 1/2 cup basic low-fat Greek yogurt

- 1 teaspoonful of honey (optional)

Instructions:

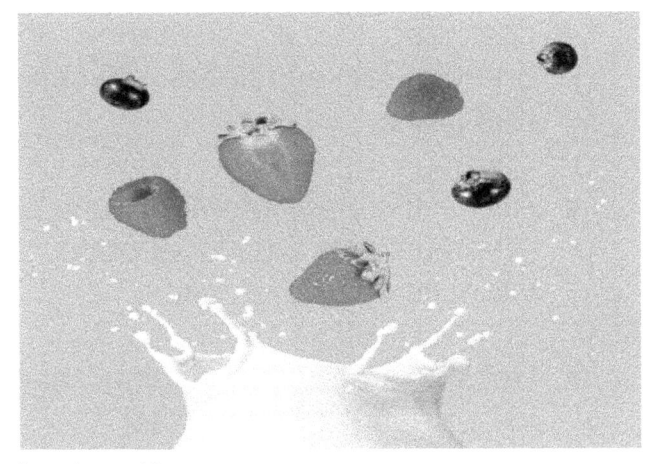

1. Put all ingredients in a blender and puree until creamy.

2. If the smoothie is too viscous, add additional coconut milk until desired consistency is achieved.

3. Strain into a tumbler and serve immediately.

Providing suggestions:

- Garnish with a few fresh

cherries or a scattering of granola for additional structure and flavor.

- Add a fistful of infant spinach or greens for an additional boost of vitamins and nutrients.

- Relish as a nourishing and invigorating breakfast or refreshment.

Benefits:

1. This smoothie is filled with antioxidants and fiber from the mixed berries, which can help decrease inflammation and promote healthy digestion.

2. Greek yogurt provides protein and probiotics, while almond milk adds healthful lipids and smoothness.

3. This recipe is a delicious and simple way to incorporate more

produce into your diet while following a gallbladder-friendly food plan.

5.4 Low-Fat Greek Yogurt with Cherries

Recipe: Low-Fat Greek Yogurt with Cherries

Ingredients:

- 1 cup low-fat Greek yogurt

- /2 cup assorted fresh berries (such as blueberries, blackberries, and strawberries))

- 1 teaspoonful of honey (optional)

Instructions:

- 1. Place the Greek yogurt into a dish.

- 2. Garnish with fresh cherries and sprinkle with honey, if preferred.
- 3. Prepare immediately.

Providing suggestions:

1. Stir in a fistful of granola or crushed almonds for additional structure and flavor.

2. Attempt different combinations of berries or other fresh fruit, such as chopped peaches or mangoes.
3. Consume as a nutritious and fulfilling breakfast, refreshment, or dessert.

Benefits:

- This preparation is high in protein and low in fat, making it a perfect choice for those following a gallbladder-friendly diet plan.

- Greek yogurt is an excellent source of calcium, which is essential for maintaining healthy bones and teeth.

- Cherries are abundant in vitamins, minerals, and antioxidants, which can help improve immunological function and decrease inflammation.

5.5 Banana Pancakes

Recipe: Banana Pancakes

Ingredients:

- 2 large bananas, mashed
- 2 eggs
- 1/2 cup wheat flour
- 1/2 teaspoon baking powder
- 1/2 teaspoon cardamom
- 1/4 teaspoon salt
- 1 teaspoonful of coconut oil or butter for heating

Instructions:

1. In a measuring dish, blend pureed bananas and eggs until well incorporated.

2. Add wheat flour, baking powder, cinnamon, and salt. Stir until a homogeneous mixture develops.

3. Place a non-stick saucepan over medium heat. Add a small quantity of coconut oil or butter to the saucepan.

4. Using a 1/4 cup measuring cup, ladle batter onto the griddle. Simmer until bubbles appear on the surface of the pancake and the sides start to dry out about

2-3 minutes.

5. Rotate the pancake and heat for an additional 1-2 minutes until golden brown.

6. Continue until all mixture is used up, adding more coconut oil or butter as required.

7. Consume heated with your preferred garnishes, such as fresh berries, low-fat Greek yogurt, or pure maple syrup.

Benefits:

- This recipe is prepared with oat flour, which is an excellent source of fiber and helps keep you feeling filled and satisfied.

- Bananas are an excellent supply of potassium, which is essential for controlling blood pressure and maintaining cardiac health.

- These pancakes are low in fat

and sugar, making them a perfect choice for those following a gallbladder-friendly diet plan.

CHAPTER SIX

6.0 Brunch Recipes for a Gallbladder Plan

When it comes to lunch choices for a gallbladder-friendly diet, it's essential to concentrate on lean protein, high-fiber carbohydrates, and healthy lipids. This can include things like roasted poultry or seafood, verdant leaves and other non-starchy vegetables, and healthful lipids like avocado or olive oil. Here are a few picnic cooking suggestions to get you started.

6.1 Roasted Chicken Pesto

Roasted chicken salad is a wonderful choice for a nutritious and satisfying supper. Here's a formula to try:

Ingredients:

- 2 boneless, skinless poultry breasts
- 1/2 teaspoon garlic powder
- 1/2 teaspoon onion powder
- Salt and pepper to flavor
- 6 cups assorted leaves
- 1 large tomato, chopped
- 1/2 cucumber, sliced
- 1/4 red onion, sliced
- 1/4 cup chopped walnuts
- 1/4 cup shredded feta cheese
- 2 tablespoons olive oil

- 2 tablespoons balsamic vinegar

Instructions:

1. Prepare your griddle to medium-high heat.

2. Season the chicken breasts with garlic powder, onion powder, salt, and pepper.

3. Broil the poultry for about 5-6 minutes per side, or until the interior temperature approaches 165°F.

4. Leave the poultry to settle for a

few minutes, then divide it into pieces.

5. In a large dish, incorporate the mixed vegetables, tomato, cucumber, and red onion.

6. Garnish the salad with sliced poultry, sliced walnuts, and shredded feta cheese.

7. In a small dish, combine the olive oil and balsamic vinegar to create a vinaigrette.

8. Sprinkle the vinaigrette over the salad, then combine everything until it's well covered.

9. Consume immediately.

This salad can be served as a standalone dinner or with a portion of whole-grain bread or biscuits. It's filled with lean protein, fiber, healthful lipids, and plenty of vitamins and minerals from the vegetables. Additionally, it's a delectable and invigorating choice for a nutritious supper.

6.2 Lentil Broth

Recipe: Chickpea Broth

Ingredients:

- 1 cup green or brown legumes
- 1 shallot, chopped
- 2 stalks garlic, chopped
- 2 carrots, sliced
- 2 bunches of celery, sliced
- 1 teaspoonful of olive oil
- 4 pints vegetable or poultry stock
- 1 teaspoon powdered cardamom
- 1 teaspoon roasted paprika
- Salt and black pepper, to flavor
- Fresh cilantro, shredded (for decoration) (for garnish)

Instructions:

1. Clean the legumes under cool water and remove them.

2. In a large saucepan, boil the olive oil over medium heat. Add the chopped onion, sliced garlic, cubed carrots, and diced celery. Simmer for about 5 minutes until the vegetables are cooked.

3. Add the legumes, water, powdered cumin, and smoked paprika to the saucepan. Bring to a simmer, then decrease the heat to medium and cover the saucepan with a covering.

4. Let the stock simmer for about 30-40 minutes until the lentils are cooked and the soup is vicious.

5. Use an immersion blender or transfer the broth to a blender and puree until homogeneous.

6. Season the broth with salt and

black pepper to flavor.

7. Serve heatedly and sprinkle with shredded fresh parsley.

This lentil broth can be served with a side vegetable or a piece of whole grain bread for a comprehensive and fulfilling dinner. Lentils are an excellent provider of fiber, protein, and different nutrients such as folate, iron, and potassium. The inclusion of vegetables like onions, garlic, carrots, and celery provides more vitamins and nutrients to the meal. The use of low-fat chicken or vegetarian stock and a minimum quantity of olive oil makes the soup healthful and low in fat.

6.3 Quinoa and Vegetable Stir-Fry

Ingredients:

- 1 cup millet
- 2 quarts water
- 1 tablespoon olive oil
- 1 red bell pepper, chopped
- 1 yellow bell pepper, chopped
- 1 small onion, chopped
- 1 small zucchini, chopped
- 1 small yellow squash, chopped
- 2 garlic cloves, minced

- 1 teaspoon chopped ginger
- 1 teaspoonful of low-sodium soy sauce
- 1 teaspoonful of rice vinegar
- Salt and pepper to flavor
- Shredded coriander (optional)

Instructions:

1. Drain the quinoa in a fine-mesh colander and add it to a medium saucepan with water. Bring to a boil, then decrease the heat to low, cover and simmer for about 15 minutes or until the water is absorbed and the quinoa is

heated through. Remove from the fire and flatten with a spatula.

2. In a large saucepan or wok, cook the olive oil over medium-high heat. Add the bell peppers, onion, zucchini, and yellow squash, and stir-fry for 5-7 minutes or until the vegetables are tender-crisp.

3. Add the garlic and ginger, and stir-fry for another minute.

4. Toss in the prepared quinoa, soy sauce, and rice vinegar. Season with salt and pepper to flavor.

5. Serve fresh, sprinkled with shredded cilantro if preferred.

This quinoa and vegetable stir-fry is a nutritious and fulfilling supper choice for a gallbladder diet. Quinoa is an excellent provider of protein, fiber, and different nutrients such as iron, magnesium, and phosphorous. The multicolored bell peppers, onion, zucchini, and golden squash provide a diversity of minerals and phytonutrients. The use of limited oil and low-sodium soy sauce makes the meal low in calories and sodium. This stir-fry can be served as a standalone meal or with a serving of sautéed vegetables for additional nutrition.

6.4 Tuna Casserole with Guacamole

Recipe: Tuna Salad with Guacamole

Ingredients:

- 1 can of mackerel, emptied

- 1 mature avocado, skinned and sliced

- 1/4 cup of chopped red scallion

- 1/4 cup of chopped carrots

- 1 teaspoonful of lemon juice

- Salt and pepper to flavor

- Optional: 1 teaspoonful of shredded fresh cilantro

Instructions:

1. In a combining dish, combine the drained tuna, sliced red onion, diced celery, and possibly shredded fresh parsley.

2. Chop the avocado into small chunks and add it to the mixture dish.

3. Sprinkle the lemon juice over the concoction and add salt and pepper to the flavor.

4. Use a spatula to carefully combine all the ingredients, being cautious not to crush the avocado too much.

5. Place the tuna salad on a bed of vegetables or whole-grain toast.

Benefits:

- Mackerel is a wonderful provider of pure protein, which is essential for developing and restoring structures in the body.

- Avocado is a healthful source of polyunsaturated lipids, which can help enhance cholesterol levels and decrease inflammation in the body.

- Red onion and celery are both rich in fiber, which can help support excellent nutrition and intestinal regularity.

- Lemon juice provides a revitalizing flavor to the meal and can help strengthen the immune system thanks to its high vitamin C content.

- This meal is a nutritious and satisfying brunch choice that can help you remain

6.5 Poultry and Vegetable Wrap

Here is a recipe for a Poultry and Vegetable Sandwich, appropriate for a gallbladder diet:

Ingredients:

- 1 whole wheat tortilla
- 2-3 ounces of grilled turkey breast, divided
- 1/4 cup of shredded carrots
- 1/4 cup of chopped zucchini
- 1/4 cup of chopped bell pepper
- 1/4 cup of assorted vegetables

- 1 teaspoonful of hummus

Instructions:

1. Place the tortilla on a level surface and distribute hummus equally over it.

2. Arrange the turkey, mixed leaves, shredded carrots, sliced cucumber, and sliced bell pepper on top of the hummus.

3. Wrap the tortilla closely around the mixture, folding in the edges as you go.

4. Divide the roll in half and serve.

This sandwich can be served with a side salad or a cup of vegetable broth. It is a nutritious and satisfying brunch choice that is high in lean protein, fiber, and important nutrients. Turkey provides nutrition without the high-calorie content of red meat, while vegetables contribute fiber, vitamins, and nutrients to the meal. Hummus provides flavor and smoothness without the need for high-fat seasonings like mayonnaise.

CHAPTER SEVEN

7.0 Supper Recipes for a Gallbladder Plan

Supper is an important food of the day as it provides the body with the necessary nutrition to power the body during relaxation. It is essential to choose meals that are simple to process and won't overburden the gallbladder. This chapter will provide some delectable supper preparations that are appropriate for a gallbladder diet.

Here are some super options for a gallbladder diet:

7.1 Grilled Mackerel with Marinated Vegetables:

Ingredients:

- 4 salmon fillets
- 2 cups of assorted vegetables (broccoli, carrots, cauliflower)
- 1 teaspoonful of olive oil
- 1 teaspoonful of chopped cilantro
- Salt and pepper to flavor

Instructions:

1. Prepare the oven to 400°F (200°C).
2. Arrange the assorted vegetables in a roasting tray and sprinkle them with olive oil.

3. Season with salt and pepper to taste and broil for 20 minutes.

4. Season the salmon fillets with salt, pepper, and preserved parsley.

5. Arrange the salmon fillets on top of the roasted vegetables and broil for an additional 15-20 minutes until the salmon is heated through.

6. Serve with a serving of brown rice or quinoa.

Benefits:

Seafood is a wonderful provider of lean protein and omega-3 fatty acids, which are important for heart and mental health. Grilled vegetables provide fiber, vitamins, and nutrients that support a healthy metabolism.

7.2 Poultry Chili:

Ingredients:

- 1 pound minced turkey
- 1 can of kidney beans, strained and washed
- 1 can of chopped tomatoes
- 1 scarlet bell pepper, sliced
- 1 scallion, sliced
- 2 cloves of garlic, chopped
- 2 tablespoons of chile pepper
- 1 spoonful of coriander
- Salt and pepper to flavor

Instructions:

1. In a large saucepan, sauté the minced turkey over medium heat.

2. Add the chopped onion and red bell pepper to the saucepan and sauté until translucent.

3. Add the chopped garlic, chile powder, cumin, salt, and pepper to the saucepan and swirl until aromatic.

4. Add the can of chopped tomatoes and strained kidney

beans to the saucepan and swirl to incorporate.

5. Decrease the heat to medium and let simmer for 20-30 minutes, whisking periodically.

6. Serve with a serving of sautéed vegetables or a small salad.

Benefits:

Turkey is a lean protein that is reduced in calories and is simple to process. Kidney beans provide fiber and nutrition that promote healthy digestion.

7.3 Roasted Chicken Breast with Sweet Potato Mash:

Ingredients:

- 4 boneless, skinless poultry breasts

- 2 sweet potatoes, scraped and chopped

- 1 teaspoonful of olive oil

- 1 sprinkle of cinnamon

- Salt and pepper to flavor

Instructions:

1. Prepare the oven to 375°F (190°C).

2. Season the chicken breasts with salt and pepper to taste and arrange them in a roasting tray.

3. Roast for 25-30 minutes, or until the poultry is heated through

7.4 Baked Mackerel with Vegetables

Ingredients:

- 4 salmon fillets
- 1 pound asparagus stalks
- 2 tablespoons olive oil
- 2 stalks garlic, chopped
- 1 teaspoonful of citrus juice
- Salt and black pepper to flavor
- Lemon slices for presentation

Instructions:

1. Prepare the oven to 400°F.
2. Cleanse the asparagus and

remove the spiny ends.

3. In a large casserole dish, combine the asparagus with 1 tablespoon of olive oil and chopped garlic. Season with salt and pepper to flavor.

4. Roast the asparagus in the preheated oven for 15-20 minutes, or until tender.

5. While the asparagus is simmering, prepare the salmon fillets. Drizzle them with the remaining tablespoon of olive oil and lemon juice. Season with salt and pepper.

6. When the asparagus is done, transfer it to one side of the roasting tray and arrange the salmon fillets on the other side.

7. Roast the salmon for 10-12 minutes, or until it separates readily with a spatula.

8. Serve the roasted salmon and asparagus with lemon slices on the side.

Benefits:

- Seafood is an exceptional provider of protein and omega-3 fatty acids, which can help decrease inflammation and promote cardiac health.

- Asparagus is rich in fiber, minerals, and antioxidants, which can support intestinal health and decrease the chance of chronic illnesses.

- Olive oil is a healthful supply of polyunsaturated lipids, which can decrease triglyceride levels and minimize the chance of cardiac disease.

7.5 Grilled Chicken with Sweet Squash

ingredients:

- 4 poultry breasts, bone-in, skin-on
- 2 large sweet potatoes, scraped and sliced
- 1 red scallion, sliced into slices
- 2 tablespoons olive oil
- 2 tablespoons garlic powder
- 2 tablespoons dried oregano
- Salt and pepper, to flavor

Instructions:

1. Prepare the oven to 375°F (190°C).

2. In a large dish, combine the sweet potatoes and red onion with olive oil, garlic powder, thyme, salt, and pepper until equally covered.

3. Distribute the sweet potatoes and red onion on a roasting sheet in a single layer. Arrange the poultry breasts on top, skin side up.

4. Roast for 35-40 minutes or until the poultry is cooked through and the sweet potatoes are succulent and golden brown.

5. Let the poultry settle for 5 minutes before serving.

Offering suggestion:

Serve the grilled chicken with sweet potato alongside sautéed green asparagus or a side salad.

Benefits:

- Chicken is a wonderful provider of pure protein, which is essential for maintaining muscular development and supporting a healthy metabolism.

- Sweet potatoes are an excellent source of fiber and phytonutrients, and they have a low glycemic index, indicating they won't cause an increase in blood sugar levels.

- Red onions contain quercetin, a plant substance with anti-inflammatory and antioxidant characteristics.

7.6 Vegetable Risotto

Ingredients:

- 1 teaspoonful of olive oil
- 1 scallion, sliced
- 2 stalks garlic, chopped
- 1 teaspoonful of chopped ginger

- 1 teaspoonful of curry masala
- 1/2 teaspoon turmeric
- 1/2 teaspoon powdered cumin
- 1/4 teaspoon powdered coriander
- 1/4 teaspoon cinnamon
- 1/4 teaspoon jalapeño pepper
- 1 can (14.5 ounces) chopped tomatoes, undrained
- 1 cup vegetable broth
- 1 sweet potato, scraped and cubed
- 1 zucchini, sliced
- 1 red bell pepper, diced
- 1 can (15 ounces) (15 oz) chickpeas, strained and washed

- 2 tablespoons green spinach stalks

- Salt and pepper to flavor

- Prepared brown rice, for serving

Instructions:

1. Melt the olive oil in a large saucepan over medium heat. Add the onion and sauté for 5 minutes or until translucent.

2. Add the garlic, ginger, curry powder, turmeric, cumin, coriander, cinnamon, and cayenne pepper to the saucepan. Whisk to incorporate and simmer for 1 minute.

3. Add the chopped tomatoes and vegetable stock to the saucepan. Reduce to a simmer and boil for 10 minutes.

4. Add the sweet potato, zucchini, and red bell pepper to the saucepan. Toss to incorporate and simmer for 20-25 minutes, or until the vegetables are cooked.

5. Add the chickpeas and vegetables to the saucepan. Toss to incorporate and simmer for 2-3 minutes, or until the spinach has softened.

6. Season with salt and pepper to flavor.

7. Serve the vegetable sauce over brown rice.

Benefits:

This vegetable curry preparation is a wonderful choice for a gallbladder-friendly supper as it is low in oil and high in fiber. The use of vegetables such as sweet potato, zucchini, red bell pepper, and spinach provides important vitamins and minerals, and the inclusion of chickpeas adds plant-based protein. The ingredients used in the masala also provide anti-inflammatory and intestinal advantages. Additionally, pairing it with brown rice provides complex carbohydrates and nutrients for a well-rounded dinner.

7.7 Marinated Scallop Skewers

Ingredients:

- 1 pound large fresh shrimp, skinned and deveined
- 1 red bell pepper, sliced and chopped into sizable chunks
- 1 yellow bell pepper, sliced and chopped into sizable chunks
- 1 green bell pepper, sliced and chopped into sizable chunks
- 1 red onion, sliced into sizable chunks
- 1/4 cup olive oil
- 2 stalks garlic, chopped
- 1 teaspoon powdered rosemary
- Salt and pepper to flavor

Instructions:

1. In a dish, combine the olive oil, chopped garlic, oregano, salt, and pepper. Blend well.

2. Add the prawns, bell peppers, and onion to the dish. Stir to cover everything in the marinate.

3. Cover and refrigerate for 30 minutes.

4. Prepare your griddle to medium-high heat.

5. Insert the shrimp, bell peppers, and onion onto skewers, alternating as you go.

6. Broil the skewers for 3-4 minutes per side, or until the shrimp is cooked through and the vegetables are slightly browned.

7. Retrieve from the griddle and serve to steam.

This recipe can be served with a side salad or couscous for a balanced dinner. The prawns provide muscularly

7.8 Roasted Bell Pepper

Ingredients:

- 4 giant bell peppers
- 1 cup prepared brown rice
- 1 cup cooked lean minced turkey
- 1/2 cup chopped onion
- 1/2 cup chopped mushrooms
- 1/2 cup shredded vegetables
- 1/2 cup shredded golden squash
- 1/2 cup tomato sauce
- 1/2 teaspoon garlic powder
- 1/2 teaspoon powdered rosemary
- 1/4 teaspoon salt
- 1/4 teaspoon black pepper

- 1/2 cup shredded low-fat cheddar cheese

Instructions:

1. Prepare the oven to 375°F (190°C).

2. Trim off the tips of the bell peppers and remove the seeds and membranes.

3. In a large dish, combine the cooked brown rice, cooked minced turkey, chopped onion, chopped mushrooms, chopped zucchini, chopped yellow

squash, tomato sauce, garlic powder, dried oregano, salt, and black pepper.

4. Insert the concoction into the bell peppers.

5. Arrange the stuffed peppers in a roasting tray and bake for 30 minutes.

6. Distribute shredded cheddar cheese over the top of the peppers and broil for an additional 5 minutes, or until the cheese is.

CHAPTER EIGHT

8.0 Appetizer Recipes for a Gallbladder Plan

Refreshments are an essential component of any diet, including a gallbladder regimen. Here are some refreshment recipes that are healthful and delicious:

8.1 Apple segments with almond butter

This lunch is simple to prepare and provides a decent blend of fiber, protein, and healthful lipids.

Ingredients:

- 1 apple
- 2 tbsp almond butter

Instructions:

1. Cleanse and divide the apple into narrow sections.
2. Sprinkle coconut butter on each piece.
3. Consume and appreciate!

Zucchini spears with hummus: This lunch is also simple to prepare and provides an excellent supply of fiber, protein, and healthful lipids.

Ingredients:

- 2 carrots
- 2 tbsp tahini

Instructions:

1. Cleanse and trim the carrots.

2. Divide them into pieces.

3. Serve with tahini for spreading.

Greek yogurt with berries: This breakfast provides an excellent amount of protein, fiber, and healthful lipids.

Ingredients:

- 1 cup low-fat Greek yogurt
- 1/2 cup assorted berries (blueberries, blackberries, strawberries)

Instructions:

1. Cleanse the berries and divide the strawberries.

2. Combine the cherries with the Greek yogurt.

Rice cake with avocado and tomato: This lunch is simple to prepare and provides an excellent blend of fiber, healthful lipids, and minerals.

Ingredients:

- 1 rice pudding
- 1/2 avocado, chopped
- 1 small tomato, chopped

Instructions:

1. Garnish the rice pudding with chopped avocado and tomato.

Air-popped popcorn: This nibble is low in calories and provides an excellent supply of fiber.

Ingredients:

- 1/2 cup air-popped popcorn
- 1 tsp olive oil
- Salt to flavor

Instructions:

1. Microwave the popcorn in an air-popper.

2. Sprinkle with olive oil and sprinkle with salt.

All of these refreshments are simple to prepare and can be savored at any time of day. They provide a decent blend of nutrition and can help you remain on schedule with your gallbladder diet.

8.2 Apple Slices with Hazelnut Butter

Here's a recipe for Apple Slices with Almond Butter:

Ingredients:

- 1 midsize mango
- 1 teaspoonful of coconut butter
- Cardamom (optional)

Instructions:

1. Cleanse the apple and divide it into pieces.

2. Distribute the almond butter on each piece of apple.

3. Sprinkle some cinnamon on top (optional)

Benefits:

- Apples are rich in fiber and contain phytonutrients that help decrease inflammation in the body.

- Macadamia butter is an excellent provider of healthful lipids and nutrients.

- Cinnamon has anti-inflammatory characteristics and may help normalize blood sugar levels.

8.3 Hummus and Celery Skewer

Here is a recipe for Hummus and Carrot Sticks:

Ingredients:

- 1 can chickpeas, drained and washed

- 2 garlic cloves, chopped

- 2 tablespoons tahini

- 3 tablespoons citrus juice
- 1/4 teaspoon salt
- 1/4 teaspoon coriander
- 3 tablespoons olive oil
- 2-3 tablespoons water
- Carrot skewers

Instructions:

1. In a food processor, incorporate chickpeas, garlic, tahini, lemon juice, salt, and cumin.

2. While the food processor is working, gently put in the olive oil and water until the combination is homogeneous and buttery.

3. Taste and modify the flavoring if required.

4. Serve the hummus with vegetable spears.

This recipe is excellent because it's high in fiber from the chickpeas and vegetables, low in cholesterol, and has a decent amount of protein from the chickpeas. Additionally, it's quick and simple to prepare, making it a perfect lunch choice.

8.4 Greek Yogurt with Almonds

Here's a recipe for Greek Yogurt with Granola:

Ingredients:

- 1 cup nonfat Greek yogurt
- 1/2 cup low-fat cereals
- 1/2 cup mixed cherries (optional)

Instructions:

1. Place the Greek yogurt into a dish.

2. Place the cereals on top of the yogurt.

3. If preferred, garnish with fresh cherries.

4. Consume as a nutritious and fulfilling refreshment.

Benefits:

- Greek yogurt is high in protein and calcium, which is important for maintaining healthy bones and muscles.

- Granola is a good source of fiber, which can help promote healthy digestion and keep you feeling full.

- Fresh berries are packed with antioxidants and vitamins, which can help boost your immune system and overall health.

8.5 Trail Mix

Here's a recipe for a simple and healthy trail mix:

Ingredients:

- 1 cup walnuts
- 1 cup almonds
- 1 cup dried cranberries

- 1 cup pumpkin seeds

- 1 cup sunflower seeds

Instructions:

1. Prepare the oven to 350°F (180°C).

2. Distribute the almonds and walnuts in a single layer on a baking sheet and roast in the oven for 10-12 minutes or until faintly toasted and aromatic. Remove from the oven and let cool.

3. In a combined dish, incorporate the roasted almonds and walnuts with the dried cranberries, pumpkin seeds, and sunflower seeds. Whisk to incorporate.

4. Separate the trail mix into individual snack-sized quantities and store them in hermetic receptacles.

5. Consume as a quick and simple breakfast on the go or as a pre-workout energy increase. This trail mix is a wonderful source of healthful lipids, protein, and fiber, making it a satisfying and nourishing nibble.

8.6 Handmade Popcorn

Here's a recipe for handmade popcorn that is an excellent nibble choice for a gallbladder diet:

Ingredients:

- 1/4 cup popcorn kernels
- 1 tbsp olive oil
- Salt to flavor

Instructions:

1. Boil a large, heavy-bottomed saucepan over medium-high fire.

2. Add the olive oil and popcorn kernels to the saucepan and swirl to cover the kernels in oil.

3. Cover the saucepan with a tight-fitting cover and jiggle the pot slightly to ensure all the kernels are saturated in oil.

4. Allow for the kernels to start bursting. Rotate the saucepan every few seconds to ensure the

popcorn doesn't brown.

5. Once the popping calms down, remove the saucepan from the heat and let it rest for a minute or two to ensure all the kernels have opened.

6. Season the popcorn with salt to flavor.

7. Offer the popcorn immediately or preserve it in a hermetic receptacle for later. Popcorn is an excellent breakfast choice because it is high in fiber and low in calories. However, be sure to monitor your serving amounts and avoid adding butter or other high-fat garnishes.

gallbladder diet:

Ingredients:

- 1/4 cup popcorn kernels
- 1 tbsp olive oil
- Salt to flavor

Instructions:

1. Boil a large, heavy-bottomed saucepan over medium-high fire.

2. Add the olive oil and popcorn kernels to the saucepan and swirl to cover the kernels in oil.

3. Cover the saucepan with a tight-fitting cover and jiggle the pot slightly to ensure all the kernels are saturated in oil.

4. Allow for the kernels to start bursting. Rotate the saucepan every few seconds to ensure the

popcorn doesn't brown.

5. Once the popping calms down, remove the saucepan from the heat and let it rest for a minute or two to ensure all the kernels have opened.

6. Season the popcorn with salt to flavor.

7. Offer the popcorn immediately or preserve it in a hermetic receptacle for later. Popcorn is an excellent breakfast choice because it is high in fiber and low in calories. However, be sure to monitor your serving amounts and avoid adding butter or other high-fat garnishes.

CHAPTER NINE

9.0 Dessert Recipes for a Gallbladder Plan

Maintaining a gallbladder diet does not mean sacrificing all your preferred delicacies. Several delectable and nutritious dessert choices are simple to prepare and gratifying. Desserts prepared with whole cereals, fresh vegetables, and low-fat dairy products are perfect for a gallbladder diet. These pastries are lower in fat and sugar, making them simpler to process and less likely to provoke gallbladder complaints.

Some popular dessert choices for a gallbladder diet include fruit dishes, roasted apples, banana pastries, and handmade sorbets. Refreshments prepared with low-fat yogurt, cottage cheese, and ricotta cheese are also excellent choices. These ingredients are high in protein, low in fat, and provide a smooth mouthfeel that is excellent for pastries.

When selecting pastries for a gallbladder diet, it is essential to pay attention to the serving amount. Moderation is crucial to preventing overloading and activating gallbladder discomfort. Below are some dessert recipes that are excellent for a gallbladder diet:

9.1 Roasted Apples with Cinnamon and Walnuts

Ingredients:

- 2 apples,
- 2 tablespoons shredded walnuts,

- 1 teaspoon cinnamon

Instructions: Prepare the oven to 350°F. Slice the apples and arrange them in a roasting tray. Distribute cinnamon and almonds over the fruits. Roast for 25-30 minutes, until the fruits are tender.

9.2 Banana Oatmeal Muffins

Ingredients: 2 large bananas, 1 cup of toasted oats, 1 sprinkle of cinnamon

Instructions:
- Prepare the oven to 350°F. Blend the bananas in a basin.
- Add the rolled oats and cinnamon and combine well.
- Place spoonfuls of the mixture onto a cookie sheet. Broil for

15-20 minutes, until the biscuits are golden brown.

9.3 Cherry Sorbet

Ingredients: 2 cups thawed mixed berries, 1/2 cup water, 1 tablespoon honey

Instructions: Transfer the frozen cherries, water, and honey to a processor.

Combine until the concoction is homogeneous. Transfer the combination into a receptacle and refrigerate for 2-3 hours, until the sherbet is solid.

9.4 Greek Yogurt with Mixed Cherries

Ingredients: 1 cup low-fat Greek yogurt, 1 cup organic cherries

Instructions: Transfer the Greek yogurt to a dish. Garnish with fresh cherries.

9.5 Strawberry Chia Pudding

Ingredients: 1/4 cup chia seeds, 1 cup unadulterated almond milk, 2 tablespoons chocolate powder, 2 tablespoons maple syrup

Instructions: Blend the chia seeds, almond milk, chocolate powder, and maple syrup in a dish. Let the concoction rest for 5-10 minutes to solidify. Serve refrigerated.

These pastries are not only delectable but also nourishing, providing a wonderful method to satiate your sugar appetite while sticking to a gallbladder-friendly diet.

Fruit Salad

Recipe for Fruit Salad:

Ingredients:

- 2 cups of fresh strawberries, cleaned and sliced
- 2 cups of fresh pineapple, sliced
- 2 cups of fresh blackberries
- 2 tablespoons of fresh blackberries
- 1 cup of fresh strawberries
- 1 teaspoonful of honey

Instructions:

- In a large dish, combine the sliced strawberries, chopped pineapple, blueberries, raspberries, and blackberries.

- Sprinkle the honey over the surface of the berries and swirl slightly to incorporate.

- Cover the dish with plastic wrap and refrigerate for at least 30 minutes to enable the flavors to blend.

- Serve refrigerated.

Cooking suggestions: Fruit salad can be served on its own as a nutritious and delightful dessert, or combined with low-fat Greek yogurt for additional nutrition and smoothness.

Benefits: This fruit salad is a delectable and nourishing dessert choice that is high in fiber, antioxidants, and minerals. The combination of different kinds of berries provides a variety of health advantages, such as improving cardiac health, decreasing inflammation, and supporting cognitive function. The inclusion of pineapple also provides a dosage of vitamin C and intestinal enzymes that may assist in absorption. The honey gives a trace of sweetness without introducing processed sugar, making this a healthier dessert choice.

9.6 Roasted Apples with Cinnamon

Recipe: Roasted Apples with Cinnamon

Ingredients:

- 4 medium-sized apples (use solid cultivars such as Granny Smith, Honeycrisp, or Braeburn)
- 1 tablespoon unadulterated butter, softened
- 2 tablespoons powdered cinnamon
- 2 tablespoons caramelized sugar
- 1/2 cup water

Instructions:

1. Prepare your oven to 375°F (190°C).

2. Clean the fruits and wipe them dry.

3. Trim off the top 1/2 inch of each apple and use a melon baller or spatula to remove the core and seeds, producing a cylindrical chamber in the middle.

4. In a small dish, combine the clarified butter, cinnamon, and brown sugar.

5. Insert the cinnamon concoction into the vacant middle of each apple.

6. Arrange the apples in a casserole dish and ladle 1/2 cup of water into the bottom of the dish.

7. Bake for 35-40 minutes, or until the apples are soft and tender.

8. Serve warm, garnished with a sprinkle of extra cinnamon if desired.

Offering suggestion:

These roasted apples can be served alone as a nutritious delicacy or can be covered with a spoonful of low-fat vanilla yogurt or whipped cream for an additional delight.

Benefits:

- Apples are an excellent source of fiber, minerals, and phytonutrients, which can help support general health.

- Cinnamon has been shown to have anti-inflammatory and antioxidant characteristics and may help normalize blood sugar levels.

- This recipe is low in fat and calories, making it a healthful dessert choice for those following a gallbladder diet.

9.7 Frozen Sorbet with Mixed Cherries

Here is a recipe for chilled yogurt with fresh cherries that is appropriate for a gallbladder diet:

Ingredients:

- 2 cups of thawed mixed berries (strawberries, blueberries, raspberries)

- 1 cup of regular low-fat Greek yogurt

- 2 tablespoons of honey

- 1 spoonful of vanilla essence

Instructions:

1. In a blender, incorporate the frozen cherries, Greek yogurt, honey, and vanilla essence.

2. Combine the ingredients until they are smooth and velvety, brushing down the edges of the blender as required.

3. Transfer the combination to a receptacle and refrigerate for at least 2 hours.

4. Retrieve the receptacle from the freezer and let it remain at room temperature for a few minutes to mellow slightly.

5. Divide the frozen yogurt into plates and serve with additional fresh cherries, if preferred.

Benefits:

- This delicacy is minimal in calories and rich in fiber and protein, making it a nutritious and fulfilling choice for those following a gallbladder diet.

- Cherries are filled with antioxidants and other advantageous nutrients that can help decrease inflammation and support general health.

- Greek yogurt is an excellent source of calcium, which is essential for bone health, and probiotics, which can promote metabolism and support immunological function.

- Honey and vanilla essence contribute natural sweetness without introducing artificial carbohydrates or dangerous lipids.

9.8 Rice Risotto with Cardamom and Raisins

Here's a recipe for rice porridge with cardamom and cranberries that works well into a gallbladder diet:

Ingredients:

- 1 cup short-grain white rice
- 2 cups water
- 1 1/2 cups unsweetened almond milk
- 1/4 cup honey
- 1/2 tsp cinnamon
- 1/4 tsp salt
- 1/4 cup currants

Instructions:

1. Clean the rice in a fine mesh colander and add it to a medium-sized saucepan with water. Bring to a simmer, then decrease the heat and cover. Simmer for 20-25 minutes, or until the water is consumed and the rice is cooked.

2. Add the coconut milk, honey, cinnamon, and salt to the saucepan with the rice. Whisk well to incorporate and bring to a simmer.

3. Decrease the heat to low and continue to simmer for 20-25 minutes, stirring periodically, until the concoction has thickened and the rice is very delicate.

4. Remove from the fire and toss in the cranberries. Leave the pudding to settle for a few minutes before serving.

5. Serve heated, covered with a

sprinkle of cinnamon and additional raisins, if preferred.

This rice pudding is a delectable and comforting delicacy that's low in cholesterol and easy on the gallbladder. It can be served on its own or with a spoonful of sweetened cream or Greek yogurt for additional creaminess.

9.9 Black Chocolate-Covered Strawberries

Certainly, here's a recipe for dark chocolate-coated strawberries:

Ingredients:

- 1 pound. fresh strawberries, cleaned and desiccated ounces.
- dark chocolate chunks or shredded dark chocolate
- 1 tsp. coconut oil (optional)

Instructions:

1. Cover a baking sheet with parchment paper and put aside.

2. In a microwave-safe dish, heat the dark chocolate chunks or powdered chocolate in 30-second increments, swirling in between until completely dissolved. If the chocolate is too viscous, add 1 tsp. of coconut oil and whisk until creamy.

3. Grasp the strawberries by the stalk and submerge them one at a time into the melted chocolate, making careful to cover them completely. Use a spatula to scrape off any leftover chocolate.

4. Arrange the chocolate-dipped strawberries on the prepared

baking sheet and let them set in the refrigerator for at least 15 minutes or until the chocolate is solid.

5. Consume immediately or preserve in a hermetic receptacle in the refrigerator for up to 3 days.

Benefits:

- Dark chocolate is rich in antioxidants and can help reduce blood pressure and enhance cardiac health.

- Strawberries are an excellent source of vitamin C, fiber, and antioxidants, which can help decrease inflammation and lower the chance of chronic illnesses.

- This delicacy is a healthier alternative to conventional chocolate desserts, as it uses dark chocolate instead of milk chocolate and organic fruit instead of manufactured ingredients.

CHAPTER TEN

10.0 Suggestions for Maintaining a Healthy Gallbladder Nutrition

Maintaining a healthy gallbladder diet is essential for those who have had their gallbladder removed or who are at risk of gallbladder problems. Here are some suggestions for maintaining a healthful gallbladder diet:

1. **Consume a variety of fruits and vegetables:** Consuming a variety of fruits and vegetables can provide you with important vitamins and nutrients that can help maintain a healthy gallbladder.

2. **Choose lean proteins:**

Selecting lean proteins such as poultry, seafood, turkey, and legumes can help decrease the chance of gallbladder difficulties.

3. **Avoid high-fat and fried foods:** Foods that are high in fat and fried can cause gallbladder problems. Avoiding these kinds of meals can help prevent gastrointestinal difficulties.

4. **Reduce your caffeine and alcohol intake:** Caffeine and alcohol can contribute to gallbladder difficulties. Reducing your consumption of these substances can help maintain a healthy gallbladder.

5. **Keep hydrated:** Consuming plenty of water and other beverages can help prevent gallstones from developing in the gallbladder.

6. **Exercise regularly:** Frequent exercise can help maintain a

healthy weight and decrease the chance of gastrointestinal difficulties.

7. **Consume small, frequent meals:** Consuming smaller, more frequent meals can help prevent gallbladder problems by decreasing the amount of labor your gallbladder has to do to process food.

8. **Preserve a healthy weight:** Being overweight or chubby can increase the chance of gastrointestinal difficulties. Maintaining a healthy weight can help decrease the chance of gastrointestinal difficulties.

9. **Contact a healthcare professional:** If you have questions about your gallbladder or have been identified with gallbladder disease, it is essential to counsel a healthcare professional for guidance on how to maintain a

healthy gallbladder diet.

10.1 Keeping Hydrated

Keeping moisturized is an essential element of maintaining a healthy gallbladder diet. Consuming enough water can help prevent the development of gallstones by preventing bile from becoming too concentrated. The standard recommendation for daily water consumption is 8-10 containers, but individual requirements may differ depending on variables such as age, exercise level, and temperature.

Other sources of hydration can include medicinal beverages, low-sugar fruit drinks, and broths. It's essential to restrict or avoid beverages with additional sugar, caffeine, or alcohol, as these can aggravate the gallbladder and exacerbate symptoms. Additionally, consuming plenty of water can help with weight management, which is another essential component in preventing gallstones.

10.2 Incorporating Physical Exercise

Incorporating physical exercise is an important component of maintaining a healthy gallbladder diet. The activity serves to maintain the digestive system functioning correctly and may decrease the chance of gallstones. Strive for at least 30 minutes of moderate physical exercise most days of the week.

Many different kinds of physical exercise can be incorporated into a healthful gallbladder diet. Some instances include:

1. **Cardiovascular activity:** This

form of exercise gets your pulse rate up and can include activities such as vigorous strolling, jogging, cycling, or swimming.

2. **Strength training:** Developing muscle through resistance training can help to improve general health and may decrease the chance of gallstones.

3. **Yoga or stretching:** Stretching and yoga can help to increase flexibility and range of motion, which can benefit digestion and general health.

It's essential to choose activities that you appreciate and that works into your lifestyle. Remember to commence gently and progressively increase the intensity and endurance of your exercises over time. If you have any health concerns, it's always a good idea to consult with your doctor before beginning a new exercise routine.

10.3 Preventing Rapid Weight Reduction or Increase

Maintaining a reasonable weight is essential for general health, including gallbladder health. Sudden weight loss or gain can increase the risk of developing gallstones, so it's essential to avoid catastrophic diets and concentrate on progressive, sustainable weight reduction if required. This can be accomplished by making minor adjustments to your nutrition and increasing physical exercise levels. Consult with a healthcare practitioner or a registered nutritionist for individualized guidance on maintaining a healthy weight and nutritional recommendations particular to your requirements.

10.4 Managing Tension

Handling stress is another essential element of maintaining a healthy gallbladder diet. Tension can contribute to intestinal difficulties and may provoke gallbladder episodes in some individuals. To handle tension, it is essential to discover healthy coping strategies such as exercise, meditation, deep breathing, and spending time with loved ones. It is also essential to prioritize self-care and make time for activities that offer pleasure and relaxation.

10.5 Routine Physical Check-Ups

It is essential to schedule frequent

medical check-ups to monitor your general health and discover any potential issues related to your gallbladder or intestinal system. Your healthcare practitioner can also provide individualized recommendations for your food and lifestyle based on your requirements and medical background. Frequent check-ups can help identify and address any problems before they become more problematic.